Contents

Democracy in Action   4

In the Hands of a Few   6

The Dawn of Citizenship   8

Imperial Rule   10

Keeping the Idea Alive   12

Struggling for Power   14

The New World   16

Change Through Revolution   18

Stirrings from Below   22

Old Nations, New Voices   24

Recognizing Women   28

Free Elections?   32

Building New Nations   34

A Voice for Everyone   36

International Involvement   40

A Right or a Duty?   44

Glossary   46

Suggested Reading   47

Web Sites   47

Index   48

Democracy in Action

I t can be easy to take the right to vote for granted, especially when we are bombarded with party political broadcasts, leaflets and posters supporting one **candidate** or another. It sometimes seems that as soon as one local or national election is over, another takes its place and another crop of posters springs up. But all of this electioneering, as well as the candidates' campaign tours, speeches, and debates, are proof that **democracy** is working and that voters have the opportunity to choose how they will be governed – and by whom.

A Long Struggle

The right to vote was not always so common, and it is still denied to people in some countries. The first governments, going back thousands of years, were formed by individuals or small groups who had the power to force their views on others. Over time, and often in the face of fierce opposition, people have fought for a fairer, more representative way of running a country. Although the struggle for the right to vote has suffered setbacks over the years, it has led to systems of government that reflect the views of the people.

The right to vote means more than simply choosing who will rule. It also enables a country to change or improve the way its government operates. Many countries follow the example of Great Britain by operating a parliamentary system. Under this kind of system, voters elect members of parliament to form the legislature; the executive is made up of the **political party** that forms a majority in the parliament, and the leader of this party usually becomes the country's **prime minister**. Other countries have a system like that of the United States, in which people elect the **executive** (in the case of the United States, the president) as well as the **legislature** (assemblies such as the US Congress). There are other systems of elected government around the world, but they all share one important feature: the people have the right to vote leaders into or out of office.

£7·99

e returned on or before

be

Right to Vote

Sean Connolly

FRANKLIN WATTS
LONDON•SYDNEY

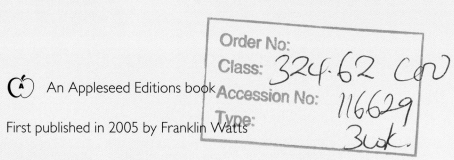

An Appleseed Editions book

First published in 2005 by Franklin Watts

Paperback edition 2007

Franklin Watts
338 Euston Road, London NW1 3BH

Franklin Watts Australia
Level 17/ 207 Kent Street, Sydney, NSW 2000

© 2005 Appleseed Editions

Appleseed Editions Ltd
Well House, Friars Hill, Guestling, East Sussex TN35 4ET

Designed by Helen James

ISBN 978 0 7496 7650 6

Dewey Classification: 324.6' 2

A CIP catalogue for this book is available from the British Library

Photographs by Corbis (Alan Schein Photography, Archivo Iconografico, S.A.,
Bettmann, Bernard Bisson/CORBIS SYGMA, Free Agents Limited, Farrell Grehan,
Dan Habib/Concord Monitor, Hulton–Deutsch Collection, Jacques Langevin/
CORBIS SYGMA, Charles & Josette Lenars, Gianni Dagli Orti, Roger Ressmeyer,
Reuters, Flip Schulke, MARC SEROTA/Reuters, Leif Skoogfors, Ted Speigel,
Stapleton Collection, Peter Turnley, Underwood & Underwood), Getty Images
(AHMAD AL–RUBAYE/AFP)

Printed in China

Franklin Watts is a division of Hachette Children's Books

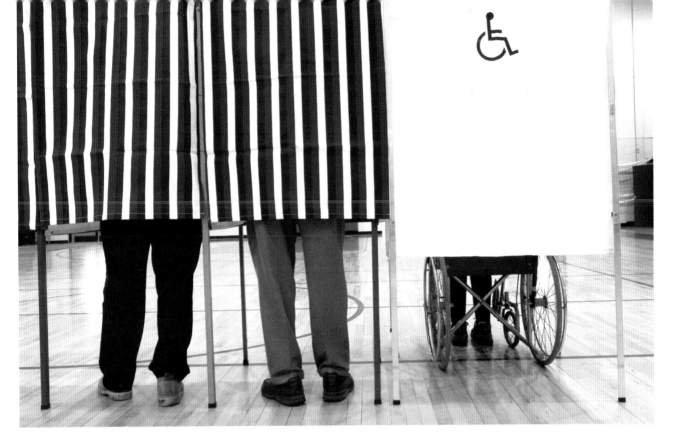

Voters mark their ballots in privacy. Today, laws in many countries dictate that handicapped voters must be able to vote easily.

'The most basic right of all was the right to choose your own leaders. The history of this country, in large measure, is the history of the expansion of that right to all of our people.'

US President Lyndon B. Johnson, 1965.

Public Servants

A true democracy would have every eligible voter casting a vote on each decision that needed to be made. This ideal, however, is unworkable in practice. In most modern democracies, people vote for candidates who will represent them in some form of legislature. These elected officials have a responsibility to represent the views of the people who voted for them — that is why they were elected. For this reason, it is common to refer to members of parliament, senators, congressmen and congresswomen, as public servants. People can consider the performance of such officials and examine their voting records and, if they are not pleased with the results, they can vote for another candidate in the next election.

In the Hands of a Few

Human beings lived together in communities for thousands of years before they learned to read and write – and leave accurate records of their lives. Nevertheless, historians and archaeologists can still find clues from this period of prehistory. Fragments of tools and weapons, coupled with cave paintings, suggest that these early people banded together for protection and to hunt and fish more effectively as teams. What the evidence cannot tell, however, is exactly how these people governed themselves. Who were the leaders of these groups of people, and how were they chosen?

Competing for Power

Experts believe they can learn more about these early people by studying primitive societies in South America, Africa and on some Pacific islands. Even today, there are communities that hunt and gather food much as the earliest humans did. These tribal people usually have a single tribal leader – someone who has proved himself to be a brave hunter or fighter. The leader's power over the community depends on his ability to provide for the people.

A tribal chief from the Pacific island of Papua New Guinea. Studying the remote societies that remain in the modern world can help explain how people governed themselves in the past.

A weak leader can be challenged and replaced. Experts suggest that the earliest societies were governed in a similar way.

The First Recorded Civilizations

By about 3000 BC, the Sumerian, Chinese, Babylonian and Egyptian civilizations had developed written alphabets. Written evidence from these peoples has shed light on how their societies operated and governed themselves.

Ancient records suggest that the rulers of these early civilizations came to power in much the same way as their prehistoric counterparts – through force. These leaders fought their rivals, gradually acquiring power over larger areas. They were supported by bands of warriors who would benefit from each victory, gaining land or money in return for their loyalty. Warriors would turn their weapons against anyone who threatened to overthrow the ruler.

What began as a single person's rise to power gradually developed into the idea of a dynasty, in which each leader passed on power to successors in his family. This gradual change in the way rulers gained and held on to power led to a number of kingdoms ruled by royal families. Even today, some countries have royal families although, in most cases, these royal leaders have no real power over their people.

A 5,000-year-old stone inscription at a temple in Ur, in modern Iraq, provides a record of ancient Sumerian government and beliefs.

Worshipping Rulers

The civilization of Ancient Egypt developed along the fertile banks of the Nile River. Egypt's rulers, the pharaohs, had an important advantage in holding on to power from one generation to the next – they were worshipped as gods. Their word was literally law, and no ordinary person could even look upon the pharaoh. Officials worked on behalf of the pharaoh, collecting grain as a form of tax from Egyptian farmers. With their great wealth, the pharaohs could order the building of magnificent temples and pyramids to worship the Egyptian gods and to protect the pharaohs' bodies for their trip to the next world.

The Dawn of Citizenship

The struggle for the right to vote has usually been linked with the struggle for democracy. Some countries, such as the United States and France, had **revolutions** in the 18th century that produced such a system of government. But the roots of democracy – like the word itself – go back to ancient Greece, about 2,500 years ago.

Competing Ideals

The rocky, mountainous landscape of Greece is not suited to widespread farming, but Greece proved remarkably fertile in other ways in ancient times. Its people produced a wealth of ideas that have survived to modern times.

Greek geography stood in the way of national unity, so the land was divided among dozens of city-states. Each was made up of a powerful city and the farming land around it. The ancient Greeks gave much thought to how their city-states should be governed. The English words 'politics' and 'police' come from the Greek word *polis*, meaning 'city'.

Many city-states developed into kingdoms, with power handed down within families. But only one of these city-states, Sparta, had a permanent army to enforce the rule of its leaders. Sparta was ruled like a modern military **dictatorship**, with

Political speeches were an important part of democracy in ancient Athens. Demosthenes (384–322 BC), who argued for action against Athens's enemies, was recognized as one of the greatest public speakers in Greece.

The ancient Greek thinker Aristotle (384–322 BC) studied the world around him to come up with new views on government and politics.

harsh punishments at home and an aggressive policy towards its neighbours.

Other city-states, notably Athens, were more open to new ideas about government. Athens had been ruled by kings and then by wealthy families known as aristocrats. Seeing that rivalries between aristocratic families were weakening Athens, single powerful rulers known as **tyrants** emerged. The modern word 'tyrant' suggests cruelty and oppression, but many Athenian tyrants had the interests of their city-state at heart.

Citizens of Athens

The Athenians believed that important decisions should reflect the interests of the city-state as a whole and not just those of a small ruling group. In about 500 BC, Athens adopted a new style of government known as democracy (from

> 'Democracy arose from men's thinking that if they are equal in any respect, they are equal absolutely.'
>
> Ancient Greek philosopher Aristotle.

Who Could Vote in Athens?

Athenian democracy was a great advance, but it actually excluded many people in the city-state from voting. Only native-born adult citizens had the right to vote. That ruled out half of the people, who were slaves. About half of the free Athenians were women, who could not be citizens. And about a third of the freemen had not been born in Athens, so they were also denied the right to vote. Despite these limitations, there were still too many eligible citizens to vote on every issue. Athens used a lottery to decide who would vote on major issues. Each lottery winner served a year as part of the Council of 500, a group that helped develop laws by advising the Popular Assembly.

the Greek words *demos*, meaning 'the people', and *kratein*, meaning 'to rule'), which involved its **citizens** in decision-making, by means of The Popular Assembly, an elected lawmaking body.

Athens flourished under its democratic government. Writers, artists, architects and scientists were attracted to the city that had become the capital of Greek culture. But powerful enemies such as the Spartans and Persians limited the independence of Athens. It eventually fell to the Romans in 146 BC. Despite its decline, however, Athens and its democratic government remained important inspirations for future political thinkers.

Imperial Rule

Ancient Rome has a reputation as a great military power, ruled with efficiency and at times without mercy. But a closer look reveals that some of the Athenian ideas about democracy survived during the long period of Roman power.

Formerly ruled by kings, Rome adopted a political system known as a **republic** in 510 BC. Republican leaders had fixed terms of office, and the ability to choose or remove them gave Romans a say in their own government. As in Athens, this was confined to citizens and excluded women and slaves. Unlike Athens, however, Rome divided its citizens into two **classes**: the patricians (noblemen) and the plebs (common people). Patricians dominated the assembly – known as the *comitia centuriata* – that made the most important decisions, especially the choosing of leaders.

Divisions and Decline

As Rome prospered, many plebs gained wealth and property. They used their power to form an assembly of their own, the *concilium plebis*, which gained power while Rome remained a republic. They also gained the right to elect **tribunes** to state their case when they felt that they had been unjustly treated by the government. Roman citizens could also elect local government representatives.

The Colosseum was built in the first century AD, after Rome had abandoned elected leaders in favour of emperors. Even during this time, some ideas of democracy remained alive at the local level.

How Do We Know?

Nearly every aspect of Roman public life was recorded, including how taxes were spent, how many eggs a military outpost ordered each month, how much foot soldiers were paid, and much more. These public records also give detailed accounts of how votes were cast in local elections and who assumed office once the votes were counted.

Other evidence gives an even better idea of what it was like to live – and vote – in ancient Rome. On the walls of buildings in Pompeii and Herculaneum, cities that were buried by the eruption of Mount Vesuvius in AD 79, many hand-painted political slogans can be found among the graffiti. One of these, which says, 'Vote for Bruttius: he'll keep local taxes down', sounds like the type of slogan a modern-day candidate would use. Apparently, day-to-day voting concerns haven't changed much – even after nearly 2,000 years.

The extensive forum of ancient Pompeii was a public place where goods were bought and sold while political ideas flowed freely.

After Rome officially became an empire in 27 BC, real power shifted to the emperor. Rome retained many of the political titles of the republican period, but elected officials could do little to influence the emperor, who remained in power for life. Even some imperial actions that seemed democratic actually served to increase the emperor's power. In AD 212, Emperor Caracalla granted Roman citizenship to all freemen living in the Roman Empire. At the time, only citizens could be forced to pay taxes, so Caracalla had simply found a new source of wealth.

Rome's political structure began to unravel as the empire declined in the fourth and fifth centuries AD. By the time Rome fell in AD 476, democratic ideals were a distant memory for many Romans.

Keeping the Idea Alive

A 14th-century German painting shows feudalism in action: the lord, knights and serfs defend Wartburg Castle against invaders.

Many people referred to the period of European history following the fall of Rome as the Dark Ages. They described the Germanic invaders who overran the empire as 'barbarians' who aimed to overthrow the social, cultural and political advances that had developed in Western Europe. Modern historians have a different view, however, believing that although many of these invaders wanted control of the land, they also wanted to enjoy the benefits of Roman society.

Feudalism and Beyond

In place of a single, unified Western empire, Europe began re-forming under different lines in the centuries following Rome's fall. Powerful kingdoms, such as France and England, began to emerge. Democracy played no real part in these places, where overall power was held by the king. The king, in turn, relied on the loyalty of noble families under a system known as feudalism. In feudalism, the king granted noblemen the right to rule their own land but, in return, the noblemen had to provide the king with troops and supplies in times of war. Peasant farmers, or serfs, lived and worked on the nobleman's land, paying him a portion of their harvest each year as a form of tax.

But this political structure was not the only system developing in Europe. Powerful cities in northern Italy and along the northern European coast began to look back to Greece and Rome to build

Medieval Florence

Medieval Florence is a good example of how democratic ideals were preserved and developed in the **Middle Ages**. Florence's **constitution** gave most of the city's political power to nine magistrates (usually called simply 'The Nine'), who were drawn mainly from the richest families in the city. The Nine would seek the advice of a group of Councillors before turning important matters over to the two councils. The Council of the People had 300 elected representatives, and the Council of the Prominent, representing richer families, had 200. Matters could become law only if they had been approved by all four groups: the Nine, the Councillors, the Council of the People and the Council of the Prominent.

Describing his city's constitution in 1439, Florentine scholar Leonardo Bruni wrote: 'Democracy also is the high respect we show, in word and in deed, for liberty, which we hold to be the end and purpose of the entire constitution.'

republican governments. Venice was established as a republic in AD 697; its leaders, or *doges*, were elected and served a fixed term. This system of government would last, with some changes, for 1,100 years. In AD 930, Iceland went even further by giving all political power to a general legislature called the Althing. This system thrived for three centuries until Iceland was taken over by Norway. The central Italian city of Florence became a republic in the 11th century. Later rulers of Florence, such as the powerful Medici family, were officially considered ordinary citizens, although they lived and ruled like kings.

This medieval painting shows an elected doge, dressed in almost regal clothing, flanked by his inner council as he decides on laws for the Venetian republic.

Struggling for Power

During the late Middle Ages, new developments gave people a greater say in government, even in countries with strong **monarchies**. Powerful English **barons** forced England's King John to sign the Magna Carta in 1215. This **charter** set limits to the king's power and paved the way for democratic advances in later centuries.

Renaissance and Reformation

The 1400s saw a movement that changed the way Europeans thought about themselves and how they should live. This period is known as the Renaissance, meaning 'rebirth'. Beginning in Italy, artists and scholars started to rediscover the legacy left by the ancient Greeks and Romans. Renaissance artists and architects studied ruins and ancient sculptures to create works of art based on mathematical ideas of harmony and proportion. Renaissance scholars reread ancient works and began to write about the importance of individuals rather than powerful institutions such as monarchies and the church. Accounts of Athenian democracy and the Roman republic inspired many Europeans to think about new forms of government.

The notion of the individual – with his or her own rights and responsibilities – also played a large part in the **Reformation**. Beginning with Martin Luther's famous protest in 1517, many European religious leaders called for a new style of worship.

The School of Athens (1509), by the great Italian artist Raphael (1483–1520), reflects the Renaissance admiration for ancient Greek philosophers such as Plato (left) and Aristotle.

Oliver Cromwell (centre) leads the Parliamentarian army to victory at the battle of Marston Moor in 1644, a turning point in the English Civil War.

They rejected the formal system of the Catholic Church, with its pope and bishops wielding great power and demanding obedience. And, while their main concern was with spiritual matters, they inspired people to question the rights of others who held absolute power, such as kings, princes and noblemen. The development of the printing press in the 16th century helped these ideas spread quickly throughout Europe.

The King is Dead

The conflict between royal power – the 'divine right' of kings to govern – and the power of elected officials erupted into violence and civil war in Britain during the 1640s. The English Parliament had been gaining power and responsibility since it formed in the 13th century. By the 17th century, it had become a powerful force, ready to assert the rights of the English people – even against their own king.

King Charles I believed in the divine right of kings and refused to compromise with Parliament.

The split led to a bitter and bloody civil war, which raged throughout Britain and Ireland. The Parliamentarians, led by Oliver Cromwell, eventually defeated the defenders of the monarchy. Charles, the opponent of democratic reform, was tried by Parliament and executed in 1649. But Britain's experiment with democracy did not last long. Cromwell assumed the title of Lord Protector and dismissed Parliament. Those who had supported Parliament in the civil war were dismayed and disappointed. In 1660, two years after Cromwell's death, Charles II (Charles I's son) was called back from exile to be crowned king. The monarchy had been restored, but on terms that were largely dictated by Parliament, which had been recalled after Cromwell's death.

The New World

By the early 16th century, European countries such as England, Spain, Portugal, France and Sweden had established **colonies** in the 'New World', as Europeans described North and South America. The type of colonies that developed reflected both the lands being colonized and the goals of the European 'mother country'. The Spanish conquered large parts of Central and South America, taking control of the Aztec and Inca civilizations with their gold and silver treasures. The French explored and claimed a large part of North America, but their settlers were mainly content to trade with local Native Americans in order to send precious furs back to Europe.

Religion and Politics

The English colonies in North America were different. Some, such as Virginia, were settled by loyalists, or colonists loyal to the English Crown and the Church of England. They were prepared to recreate English society in North America and to obey the bishops and other officials of the established English church.

All 41 adult male Pilgrims signed the Mayflower Compact in 1620, marking the first move toward self-government in an English colony in North America.

The **Puritans** and other colonists, known as 'Pilgrims', who settled in Massachusetts had different ideas. They disagreed with the religious system in England and had already fled their home country to find refuge in the Protestant Netherlands. They arrived in North America intending to worship and lead their lives away from the watchful eye of the English Crown and its religious representatives.

Soon after making landfall – and before they moved on to found Plymouth – the Pilgrims signed the Mayflower Compact in 1620. Taking its name from the ship that had transported the 102 settlers, this document is often referred to as the first written constitution in North America. It described the settlers as a political group with the power to create and enforce laws concerning the general good of the new settlement. In signing the compact, the Pilgrims took the first step in a series of actions that would lead to the creation of the US Declaration of Independence more than 150 years later.

Rather than receive and obey orders passed down from English bishops, the New England settlers made their own choices regarding how they would worship. Many decisions, including who should have which land and who should become minister, were determined by the communities in regular meetings. Many New England communities still arrive at decisions in such town meetings.

New England Town Meetings

New England town meetings are often described as the best examples of democracy in action. During these gatherings, usually held annually, the taxpayers in a town meet to discuss and agree upon how local taxes should be spent for the next year. Everyone has a say in the discussion, and opinions often differ sharply on some points – whether to give the firefighters a pay rise or to spend the money on a new school gym, whether to paint the town hall or to add a new set of traffic lights. Those taking part in the debate are carrying on the tradition of the 16th-century New Englanders, but a citizen of ancient Athens would also be familiar with the process – if not the points being debated.

A taxpayer waits his turn to make a point at a New Hampshire town meeting while other townspeople listen.

Change through Revolution

Changes in society sometimes come about over long periods of time through a series of small measures. Societies undergoing such changes are said to be evolving. But there are also times when evolutionary change is not rapid enough for some people, who choose instead to chart a revolutionary course.

The long struggle for representative democracy, which is at the core of the struggle for the right to vote, has seen both types of change. The development of democracy in ancient Athens was evolutionary: successive generations of Athenian leaders altered the system gradually to give their citizens more of a say in how Athens was governed. Sixteenth-century England, on the other hand, had a form of revolution when it erupted in civil war, leading to the execution of the king and rule by Parliament. The late 18th century saw two other famous revolutions – in the United States and in France – which have had long-lasting effects in both their own countries and the world at large.

'No Taxation Without Representation'

During the 17th and 18th centuries, Great Britain's 13 colonies along the eastern coastline of North America gained a measure of self-government. Although still part of the growing British Empire, they had their own assemblies (usually modelled on the English Parliament) and were responsible for much of their own business, including overseeing judges and raising taxes and armies. Britain accepted this arrangement because goods from the colonies brought wealth to the mother country.

The French and Indian War (1754–1763) changed the political and economic shape of North America. Britain's victory removed French control from North America, but this victory came at an enormous financial price. In order to

The BLOODY MASSACRE perpetrated in King — Street BOSTON on March 5th 1770 by a party of the 29th REGt.

Unhappy BOSTON! see thy Sons deplore,
Thy hallow'd Walks besmear'd with guiltless Gore:
While faithless P—n and his savage Bands,
With murd'rous Rancour stretch their bloody Hands;
Like fierce Barbarians grinning o'er their Prey,
Approve the Carnage and enjoy the Day.

If scalding drops from Rage from Anguish Wrung
If speechless Sorrows lab'ring for a Tongue,
Or if a weeping World can ought appease
The plaintive Ghosts of Victims such as these;
The Patriot's copious Tears for each are shed,
A glorious Tribute which embalms the Dead

But know FATE summons to that awful Goal,
Where JUSTICE strips the Murd'rer of his Soul:
Should venal C—ts the scandal of the Land.
Snatch the relentless Villain from her Hand,
Keen Execrations on this Plate inscrib'd,
Shall reach a JUDGE who never can be brib'd.

Engrav'd Printed & Sold by PAUL REVERE BOSTON

The unhappy Sufferers were Messrs. SAMl. GRAY SAML. MAVERICK, JAMS. CALDWELL, CRISPUS ATTUCKS & PATk. CARR
Killed. Six wounded; two of them (CHRIST. MONK. & JOHN CLARK) Mortally

This engraving shows British soldiers opening fire on unarmed Bostonians in 1770 in what came to be known as the 'Boston Massacre'. Although the truth was somewhat different – the soldiers had been violently provoked and were later tried for murder – the incident highlighted the strong anti-British feelings of American colonists.

gain back some of this cost, Parliament in London established a series of acts designed to raise tax money in North America. Legislation such as the Stamp Act (1765) and the Townshend Acts (1767) proved very unpopular with the American colonists. Angry Americans thought it was unfair that they should be taxed without having any elected representatives in Parliament to state their case.

It was this sentiment, given expression in the familiar cry 'No Taxation Without Representation', that boosted the notion that the colonies must be independent if they wanted to have any real say in how they were governed. What began as a rebellion to preserve the rights spelled out in the Mayflower Compact became a full-scale war for independence. One of its main supporters was Englishman Thomas Paine. In his 1776 pamphlet 'Common Sense',

The American Revolution paved the way for greater voting rights for Americans, but it had little immediate effect on ordinary people. Historians estimate that only six per cent of the adult male population in the US was entitled to vote at the time the Constitution was written.

Paine wrote, 'For in absolute government the king is law, so in free countries the law ought to be king, and there ought to be no other.'

Freedom and Terror

The second great 18th-century revolution took place in France. There, the vast majority of the people had even less representation than the rebellious American colonists had. By 1789, though, a series of costly wars had forced King Louis XVI to summon the Estates General, a type of parliament. Three **estates** were represented in this body: the First Estate (clergy), the Second Estate (noblemen) and the Third Estate (common people). Regulations gave equal voting power to each estate, even though the first and second estates represented only a tiny **minority** of the country. Encouraged by new ideas of liberty, representatives of the Third Estate signed an oath pledging to push for a National Assembly, in which every representative would have one vote.

France could not be governed until this dispute was resolved, and the king sent troops to force the National Assembly to back down. News of this action swept through France and, on July 14, 1789, angry Parisians stormed the Bastille prison, the symbol of royal power. The French Revolution had begun.

'The right of voting for representatives is the primary right by which other rights are protected.'

Thomas Paine in his Dissertation on First Principles of Government, 1795.

'Law is the expression of the general will. Every citizen has a right to participate personally, or through his representative, in its foundation.'

Part of the 'Declaration of the Rights of Man', approved by the French National Assembly, August 1789.

Revolutionary artist Jean-Pierre Houel painted Storming the Bastille *just weeks after the prison had fallen in 1789.*

The Age of Enlightenment

The dramatic advances in mathematics and science – led by Galileo Galilei, René Descartes and Isaac Newton – that took place during the 17th century helped shape the way educated people thought in the 18th century. People had begun to unravel some of the mysteries of nature and were confident that they could discover the scientific principles that underpin everything in the universe. They saw human **reason** as the key to understanding these questions. This faith in human reason inspired many writers and philosophers, such as Germany's Immanuel Kant and a group of French writers led by Voltaire, Denis Diderot and Jean-Jacques Rousseau. These thinkers believed that reason and understanding – and therefore progress – depended on human liberty. The views developed during this period, known as the Age of Enlightenment, also inspired the struggle for freedom and democracy.

The original goals of the National Assembly were set out in August 1789 in a document known as the 'Declaration of the Rights of Man'. This political document enshrined the notions of equality and freedom that would eventually become cornerstones of the French government. Over the next few years, the National Assembly (sometimes changing its name) became the most powerful governing force in France. Revolutionary leaders such as Georges Danton and Maximilien Robespierre clashed with those who opposed change – and often with each other. Louis XVI was executed in 1793, ushering in a period known as the Reign of Terror, when many people died at the **guillotine**. After years of turmoil, many French people began calling for a strong leader who could rule France efficiently, but who would also respect the basic goals of the Revolution. In 1799, just such a man appeared on the scene – Napoleon Bonaparte.

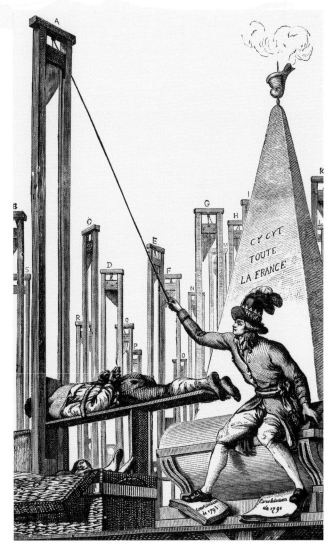

An illustration criticizing the excesses of the French Revolution depicts Maximilien Robespierre hard at work in a sea of guillotines, waiting to execute his enemies.

Stirrings from Below

At the beginning of the 19th century, wealthy landowners still held power in Europe. And although the US Declaration of Independence had stated that 'all men are created equal', a similar minority enjoyed real power in America. On both sides of the Atlantic, the only people who had the right to vote were men with considerable wealth. At the same time, however, less wealthy people – farmers, labourers, and mechanics – began to question a system that left them without a real voice in government. Gradually, their voices brought new freedom to the voting system.

Voting rights in European countries were decided on a national level, so that all of Britain or France had the same system. It was hard to take power from the small groups that elected their own people in these countries. The American system worked differently, with each state deciding who should have the right to vote within that state. The country was expanding, with new western territories becoming states. The people who decided on voting rights in these states were not rich landowners, but frontiersmen and small farmers. Between 1812 and 1821, six western territories became states. Each gave the right to vote to all white adult men. Their example encouraged activists in other states to change voting laws. By 1860, nearly every state had given the vote to all white men.

British Reform

Great Britain had also recognized the demands for greater voting rights, and its government did not want to risk a revolution by failing to act. In the 19th century, Parliament passed three Reform Acts to make voting more democratic. The 1832 act tripled the number of people who were entitled to vote. Changes also took place elsewhere in the British Empire. Voting laws in Canada became freer in 1840, when the Act of Union united the separate Canadian colonies as the Province of Canada. The colonies (now states) of Australia gained new constitutions in the 1840s, extending the vote to adult men. Similar voting rights were established in New Zealand after it signed its first constitution in 1852.

Soldiers sweep through an 1819 demonstration calling for political reform in Manchester, England, killing several in what later became known as the Peterloo Massacre.

Showdown in Rhode Island

In October 1841 in the US, Thomas Dorr, a Rhode Island state representative, organized an unofficial meeting that drafted a state constitution known as the 'People's Charter'. The charter gave the vote to all white males aged 21 or older. Two separate elections were held in April 1842. Landowning voters elected Samuel Ward King as governor, while those who owed their right to vote to the charter chose Dorr.

In June 1842, with the support of 3,000 followers and two stolen cannons, Dorr set out to disarm King's 'illegal' government. He was unlucky. The stolen cannons were old and rusty and failed to fire. His supporters drifted away, and Dorr was arrested and convicted of **treason**. He spent two years in prison, but the words he spoke in court are still remembered: 'The servants of a righteous cause may fail or fall in the defense of it. But all the truth that it contains is indestructible.'

Old Nations, New Voices

The first Europeans to gain voting rights were already powerful. It was the English barons, after all, who had forced King John to grant them more rights in the Magna Carta in the 13th century (see page 14), so the precious right belonged to a very small minority.

Over time, such powerful minorities had to recognize the growing influence of other social groups, just as King John had been forced to deal with the barons. The rise of commerce in the late Middle Ages led to a growing middle class of merchants, who pressed for voting rights to match their new position in society. By the 19th century, labourers (the working class) were eager to have their say in society. By organizing themselves in **unions** and threatening to withhold their labour, they gained the power to push through their demands. As a result, more working-class people (although still only men) gained the right to vote.

Peasants in late 19th-century Russia were free in theory but, in reality, they had almost as little say in Russian government as their grandparents had had as serfs.

Those Who Are Apart

Even as the number of new voters began gradually to increase, there were some societies in which those in power saw another group as inferior and therefore incapable of making sensible judgments in the voting booth.

The mid-19th century saw two of the world's most powerful countries – the United States and Russia – torn apart by such a view. In the United States, the practice of slavery meant that millions of African-Americans were seen as property – living machines to do the work of their owners. And in Russia, an even larger number of people, called serfs, were also considered the property of wealthy landowners. Neither of these groups had the right to vote.

A Broken Promise?

Despite the founding fathers' assertion that 'all men are created equal', slavery existed in the United States until the mid-19th century. Abolitionists, or people who opposed slavery, argued that African-American slaves, who made up about one-eighth of the US population, should be free citizens just like white people. Supporters of slavery, mainly in the southern states, triggered the Civil War in order to preserve their 'right' to own slaves.

African-American slaves pose outside their living quarters on a farm in Cockspur Island, Georgia, during the Civil War.

Russian public opinion turned sharply against the Czar after government troops brutally crushed a peaceful pro-democracy demonstration in 1905.

The eventual defeat of the South marked the end of slavery. The 13th **Amendment** to the Constitution, ratified in December 1865, outlawed slavery throughout the country. And the 15th Amendment, ratified five years later, granted full voting rights to all American men, including former slaves.

'The parties that made the Constitution aimed to cheat and defraud the slave, who was not himself a party to the compact or agreement.'

Frederick Douglass, escaped slave and leading abolitionist, in his essay 'The Constitution and Slavery', 1849.

Unfortunately, some states imposed restrictions that made it impossible for African-Americans to vote, or even to qualify to vote. Measures such as 'grandfather clauses' (restricting the vote to those whose grandfathers had been able to vote – mainly white people), **poll taxes** and **literacy tests** meant that only those with enough education or money could vote. Some of these measures lasted well into the 20th century.

Following decades of campaigning, Russia's serfs were freed in 1861. But like America's former slaves, these newly freed Russians had little chance to improve their living conditions by voting. In fact, very few Russians had any voice in their government, in which the Czar held ultimate power. The system of denying people a political voice in matters finally backfired when Russia was torn apart by revolution in 1917.

Native Peoples

The United States, Canada, Australia and New Zealand developed because of large-scale **immigration**. But the original inhabitants of these countries often suffered as a result. They lost most of their land to the new settlers and were denied full citizenship and voting rights in the new countries.

Groups of Native Americans in the United States were treated as separate nations living within the US until the early 20th century. In 1924, Congress finally granted US citizenship – and full voting rights – to the Native American population. Canada's native people were denied the right to vote when the Canadian colonies united in 1867. This made it hard for them to argue their case in a number of controversial issues involving land rights. After a spirited campaign, they were granted the right to vote across Canada in 1960.

Australia's Aboriginal people secured the right to vote in several Australian colonies in the 19th century, but a series of laws in the early 20th century denied non-white people (including Aborigines) this right. They eventually secured the right to vote in federal elections in 1962 and, five years later, they finally gained full citizenship.

New Zealand's Maori men technically received the right to vote, along with white men, in 1853. But this right was limited to property owners, and the Maori people did not believe in private ownership of land. In 1867, Maori men got the right to vote for their own candidates, with the winners taking the four seats in the New Zealand Parliament that were set aside for Maori people. This system remains in place today. Ninety-five of the 99 members of the House of Representatives are elected by 'European' (non-Maori) voters, and the other four are elected by voters who are at least half-Maori.

Recognizing Women

By the 19th century, when the issue of voting rights (for the poor, immigrants, racial minorities and others) was hotly debated around the world, women turned their efforts to achieving the same right for themselves. Many women had been at the forefront of the struggle to gain the vote for ethnic groups in their own countries. Their work had been an enormous sacrifice, since they themselves could not vote. With the vote, women argued, they would be able to shape the course of the future – and, ideally, make it fairer.

Progress and Disappointment

When voting rights had been extended throughout Europe and into the New World in the 17th and 18th centuries, women had not been accorded the right to vote. There were some exceptions, however. The British colonies of North America, for example, followed the British practice of allowing the vote only to property owners. In some of these colonies, female property owners had the same voting rights as their male counterparts.

Women rallied to the cause of the French Revolution in the 1790s in an effort to promote gender equality as well as increased democracy.

But landowning American women found that the right to vote was denied them once the United States became independent. US measures to make the right to vote fairer – especially by removing the property-owning qualification – actually removed the only means American women had to vote.

The rallying cry of the French Revolution had been 'Liberty, Brotherhood, and Equality'. Some French women argued that this call should include women. In 1791, an actress named Olympe de Gouges published 'The Declaration of the Rights of Women and Citizenesses'. But her fellow (male) revolutionaries, who were drawing up a new constitution, did not prove revolutionary enough to include women in it. The new constitution gave the vote to all adult men. Women were expected to continue with their traditional roles and remained dependent on men.

Elizabeth Cady Stanton holds her daughter Harriet, who later followed in her mother's footsteps in the fight for women's rights.

An International Movement

At the beginning of the 19th century, women had actually lost ground in their struggle for the right to vote. New laws widening the right to vote were targeted only at men, and women were strictly denied voting rights in those places where loopholes had previously allowed them to vote. Things soon began to change, however, helped by advances in communications (such as the invention of the telegraph) and in travel (train networks began to span even the largest countries). For the first time, American women were able to join forces to improve their position in society.

'We hold these truths to be self-evident: that all men and women are created equal.'

Elizabeth Cady Stanton, rephrasing the famous lines of the US Declaration of Independence: 'We hold these truths to be self-evident, that all Men are created equal.'

Feminists such as Lucretia Coffin Mott, Elizabeth Cady Stanton, Susan B. Anthony, Lucy Stone, Abby Kelley Foster and Ernestine Rose – all of whom had campaigned against slavery – led the calls for woman **suffrage**. They were joined by prominent American men, including clergymen Henry Ward Beecher and Wendell Phillips and essayist and poet Ralph Waldo Emerson.

Britain's 'Suffragettes'

British feminist Mary Wollstonecraft published *A Vindication of the Rights of Woman* in 1792. This work inspired 19th-century feminists to argue for increased rights for women while at the same time campaigning for an end to slavery and for improved education and living conditions for the poorest members of society. Despite support from some statesmen and social writers such as John Stuart Mill, John Bright and Richard Cobden, the suffragists were blocked by Queen Victoria and the long-serving Prime Ministers Benjamin Disraeli and William Gladstone. Critical commentators called them 'suffragettes', a term that made the movement seem dainty and not quite serious.

The suffragists responded by merging various feminist groups to form the National Union of Woman Suffrage Societies in 1897. In 1903, Emmeline Pankhurst decided that this group was too weak and set up a more militant breakaway group, the Women's Social and Political Union. Their **boycotting**, picketing and other high-profile activities kept the suffrage issue at the forefront of British politics. As World War I (1914–18) ended, Parliament was finally swayed by the suffragists' arguments, granting women aged 30 and older the vote. Ten years later, this age was dropped to 21, giving women complete voting equality with men.

Emmeline Pankhurst (centre) leads a procession of nearly 50,000 women through London in 1915 to demand a greater role for women in the World War I effort.

Recognizing Women

Like their American counterparts, women in Canada, Australia and New Zealand had been active in civil rights campaigns long before they gained the right to vote. As part of the British Empire, they fought to end the slave trade in the early 19th century, and they also tried to improve the legal position of native people in their own countries.

Getting the Message

During the second half of the 19th century, women began to make gains. The first American success came in 1889, when Wyoming granted women full voting rights. Four years later, New Zealand became the first country to grant women the right to vote. And in 1894, South Australia, which was still a separate British colony, passed a law guaranteeing woman suffrage. All Australian women got the right to vote when the separate colonies united to form the Commonwealth of Australia in 1901.

More American states granted women the right to vote in the late 19th and early 20th centuries. With each success, the calls grew louder to amend the US Constitution, thereby forcing every state to follow these examples. Such a move eventually came in 1920, when the 19th Amendment made female voting a constitutional right.

Most other countries passed laws granting voting rights to their women citizens over the course of the 20th century. By the end of the century, a number of women – including Golda Meir of Israel, Indira Gandhi of India, Margaret Thatcher of the United Kingdom, and Corazon Aquino of the Philippines – had held the highest elective office in their countries. The long struggle had shown some real results.

British suffragist Emmeline Pankhurst took her message across the Atlantic to address 5,000 supporters in Boston, Massachusetts.

Nineteenth-century advocates of women's suffrage often had to deal with angry – and sometimes violent – criticism from the men who attended their meetings. Meetings were also often disrupted by gangs of street bullies. Once, when Susan B. Anthony spoke in Albany, New York, the mayor sat beside her holding a revolver to discourage possible attacks by hoodlums in the audience.

Free Elections?

World War I ended in 1918. At least 10 million soldiers had died in battle, and the world was weary of fighting. US President Woodrow Wilson described it as 'the war to end all wars', meaning that it had resolved some of the disputes that had divided the world for so long. And with European monarchies being replaced by democratically elected governments, many people had reason to agree with the president.

But other, less representative, governments also emerged in the years following World War I. **Fascist** governments emerged in Italy and Spain, as well as in Germany (ruled by the fascist-style Nazi Party) and Japan. Fascist governments believed in the virtue of war, an aggressive attitude that led to the outbreak of World War II (1939–45).

Totally opposed to the fascists, but in effect even more powerful, were the **communist** governments that sprang up in Eastern Europe and China after World War II. Claiming to be ruled by the working people, these governments called themselves democracies. But in reality, their populations had no say in how their countries were governed. Only members of the ruling party

A young Chinese pro-democracy protester waves a rifle defiantly in Tiananmen Square, Beijing, in June 1989. Chinese soldiers crushed the demonstration, killing between 1,500 and 4,000 protesters.

The International Verdict

Foreign election observers visiting troubled countries can offset government intimidation of opposition parties before an election. Likewise, the opposition can derive comfort if observers condemn conditions leading to a government victory.

'The conditions for credible democratic elections do not exist in Zimbabwe at this time,' the US-based National Democratic Institute for International Affairs (NDI) said in the weeks before Zimbabwe's parliamentary elections in 2000. Former Nigerian Vice President Alex Ekwueme, who led the NDI team on a pre-election mission, said: 'The violence has created an atmosphere of fear and anxiety.' Robert Mugabe's ruling party won these disputed elections, but the opposition party took some comfort. The international verdict on the elections proved that they had not been fair and gave opposition groups hope that they might eventually win in a fair fight.

could run as political candidates, and the governments used their so-called election victories to proclaim how popular they were. Those who protested – whether in fascist or communist countries – were often imprisoned or executed.

The Effect on Voting

The fascists and their allies were defeated during World War II. And in the years since the war, nearly every communist government has been replaced. By 1991, even the most powerful communist country, the Soviet Union, had abandoned that form of government in favour of Western-style democracy.

But many other countries use the same brutal tactics to control their population and to make voting meaningless. Iraq, under Saddam Hussein, described itself as a republic, but the Iraqi police and army stifled opposition to the ruling Baathist Party. Throughout his rule, Saddam Hussein boasted of nearly 100 per cent support in elections, but ordinary Iraqi people knew the price they would pay – imprisonment or execution – if they opposed him. President Robert Mugabe of Zimbabwe (also a republic) continues to use similar tactics to intimidate opposition voices. In such countries, the government opposes a **free press** so that the people remain ignorant of anti-government opinion. The main weapon in such dictatorships is fear, the real enemy of democracy.

'Ignorance is an evil weed, which dictators may cultivate among their dupes, but which no democracy can afford among its citizens.'

W. H. Beveridge (1879–1963), British economist.

Building New Nations

When World War II ended in 1945, many countries that had been occupied by Nazi Germany and Japan were set free. People in European countries such as France, Belgium and Norway were once again able to choose their own governments by voting in elections. But many of the lands that had been attacked by the Japanese – places such as India, Burma and Indochina – were still colonies controlled by European nations. The people in these colonies wanted the right to change their governments through elections.

Independence movements formed in Asia, Africa and the Caribbean region. Over three decades, these movements dismantled nearly the entire colonial network. Sometimes the path to independence was peaceful. Formerly British, India and Pakistan were formed as independent countries in 1947. Mahatma Gandhi, the Indian leader who had campaigned peacefully for independence for decades, became a model for independence movements in many other countries. Ghana became the first African country south of the Sahara Desert to gain full independence from Great Britain in 1957. France recognized the independence of Côte d'Ivoire (Ivory Coast) in 1960.

'I have cherished the ideal of a democratic and free society in which all persons live together in harmony and with equal opportunities. It is an ideal which I hope to live for and to achieve. But if needs be, it is an ideal for which I am prepared to die.'

Nelson Mandela, speaking at his own trial in 1964.

Other independence movements faced bitter opposition. Some 11,000 people died in guerrilla fighting in Malaysia before it gained independence in 1957. Algeria and the Congo both struggled through bitter and bloody fighting before they gained independence in the early 1960s.

Stubborn Resistance

Some African governments, representing the small landowning minority, saw the independence movement as a threat. The most famous example of such a

government was that of South Africa, which enshrined racial discrimination in a system of laws known as **apartheid**.

Under the apartheid system, South Africa's white citizens (making up about one-fifth of the overall population) denied black South Africans (about two-thirds of the population) and other non-white groups many basic rights. Education and health care were poor, and the majority of South Africans did not have the right to vote to improve their own living conditions.

The African National Congress (ANC), a non-violent civil rights organization founded in 1912, campaigned for wider voting rights for all South Africans. When stricter apartheid laws went into effect in 1948, the ANC began to operate as a secret organization, often clashing with the South African police. In 1964, ANC leader Nelson Mandela and 10 other anti-apartheid activists were sentenced to life in prison. By that time, though, these leaders – especially Mandela – had supporters around the world. Their assistance, coupled with Mandela's determination not to abandon his struggle even in prison, helped overturn apartheid. In 1990, Mandela was released and, in 1994, he was elected president in South Africa's first election open to all citizens.

Young South Africans demonstrate in favour of democratic, non-racial elections in the late 1980s, the last years of apartheid.

35

A Voice for Everyone

By the 1960s, many countries had political systems that guaranteed all of their adult population the right to vote. But in practice, many groups still found it difficult to exercise this right. Some of the obstacles were tied in with broader civil rights issues, such as those concerning African-Americans and other ethnic groups in the United States. Others related to people whose language problems or physical disabilities left them unable to cast a vote. With the social climate more responsive to debate and change, some people began to question the basic premise of electoral law in the US.

Removing the Final Obstacles

African-Americans had been granted the right to vote in 1870, but some states, mainly in the South, continued to make it difficult for blacks to register to vote. In most parts of the country, registering to vote was a straightforward process that involved completing basic forms. But in some states, black people had to interpret complicated sections of the state's constitution (to demonstrate their political awareness) or pay a poll tax of up to half a week's wages before they

African-Americans line up to register to vote in 1961 as widespread civil rights voter registration drives begin to take effect in the American South.

'Freedom Summer'

Bob Moses, an African-American native of New York, travelled to Mississippi in 1961 as part of the Student Nonviolent Coordinating Committee (SNCC) voter registration drive. The drive faced hostility from local white people, and often members were arrested or beaten by local police officers. Despite being stabbed by three white men – and then finding the local courthouse 'closed for the afternoon' when he tried to report the crime – Moses was determined to continue. But by mid-1964, the SNCC efforts had added only 4,000 new registered voters. Moses invited 900 additional volunteers in a project that was called Freedom Summer. Three volunteers – two white and one black – were killed at the start of the summer, causing the national media to follow the voter registration drive intently. The tragic casualties, coupled with the violence surrounding the civil rights marches in Selma, Alabama, in 1965, boosted support for the legislation that eventually became the Voting Rights Act of 1965. Unita Blackwell, who registered to vote in 1964, explained: 'For black people in Mississippi, Freedom Summer was the beginning of a whole new era. People began to feel that they weren't just helpless anymore.'

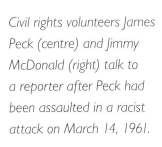

Civil rights volunteers James Peck (centre) and Jimmy McDonald (right) talk to a reporter after Peck had been assaulted in a racist attack on March 14, 1961.

'The law down here is law made by white people, enforced by white people, for the benefit of white people. It will be that way until the Negroes begin to vote.'

Civil rights worker Bob Moses describing conditions in Mississippi after he was attacked in 1961.

could register. Meanwhile, whites in the same community could simply sign their name to be registered. In some parts of the South in the early 1960s, fewer than 40 per cent of black adults were registered to vote. In Mississippi, only 6.4 per cent of blacks were registered.

Inspired by campaigners such as Dr Martin Luther King, Jr., and Malcolm X, and by several Supreme Court rulings outlawing **segregation** in the 1950s, civil rights workers flooded into the South to mobilize the black vote. Volunteers from groups such as the SNCC went door to door to get people to register. They often faced physical abuse from white people opposed to their efforts.

In February 1965, Jimmie Lee Jackson, a volunteer from Marion, Alabama, was killed in Selma, Alabama. Civil rights activists decided to draw national attention to their struggle by organizing an 80-kilometre march from Selma to Montgomery, the state capital. The march began as scheduled on March 7, but the 600 marchers were stopped when Selma's sheriff and 200 troopers blocked their way at a bridge. When the marchers refused to turn back, the officers attacked with whips, clubs and tear gas. Seventeen marchers were sent to the hospital as a result of this violence. But the events were seen across the nation on television news broadcasts. Two weeks later, the march went ahead, this time with federal protection.

Dr Martin Luther King, Jr., led the 1965 civil rights march from Selma to Montgomery, Alabama. Marchers were attacked by police outside Selma in an incident remembered as 'Bloody Sunday'.

A Voice for Everyone

The march helped the behind-the-scenes negotiations conducted by Dr King and other civil rights leaders in Washington. In August 1965, Congress passed the Voting Rights Act. The Act ended literacy tests and gave federal officials the right to investigate voter registration practices, making it a criminal offence to interfere with any of the voting rights granted by law. Backing up the new law was the 24th Constitutional Amendment, which outlawed poll taxes in any federal election.

Widening the Act

The eventual success of the civil rights movement in the 1960s inspired people to call for other sweeping changes in the United States and other countries. Many Americans staged large-scale protests against the war in Vietnam. Thousands of soldiers and civilians were dying in a conflict that many believed was wrong. Many of the American dead were soldiers as young as 19. Young Americans argued that they were being called on to die for their country at a time when – because the voting age was 21 – they were too young to have a say in the country's government.

Thousands of Americans protested against the Vietnam War, in which half of the young men killed were not old enough to vote.

Young Americans were inspired by Britain's 1969 Representation of the People Act and similar laws in Canada and Australia, which reduced the voting age to 18. In 1970, the US Voting Rights Act, which had been passed as a civil rights measure, was extended to grant the vote to 18-year-old Americans in federal elections. The 26th Amendment, ratified in 1971, guaranteed this right in state and local elections as well.

The Voting Rights Act was amended twice more, in 1975 and 1982. Later changes included requiring **bilingual** ballots in some counties and enforcing a permanent ban on literacy tests. Federal law now allows voters who are illiterate, blind or disabled to be assisted in the voting booth by a person of their own choosing.

International Involvement

The face of world politics has changed much since the end of World War II. One of the lasting achievements of the postwar years has been the role of the United Nations (UN), which was formed in the last months of the war. The United Nations stands as an international organization devoted to peace and development. Ideally, it offers a chance for countries to settle their differences in a public arena, rather than resorting to military action.

The United Nations also offers countries a voice in world affairs in the same way that elections provide voters with a chance to have a say in their government. Without an international body such as the UN, smaller, less wealthy countries would be nearly powerless to shape world events. But within the **General Assembly** – and even more importantly, when they get a turn on the **Security Council** – nations can offer their point of view. Very often, important UN votes are decided by majorities of only two or three countries. In such a system, Trinidad and Malawi are as important as the United States and China.

The flags of member nations fly outside the United Nations General Secretariat Building in New York City.

UN peacekeepers, recognizable by their familiar blue helmets, try to restore peace in war-torn Bosnia, 1995.

The Groundwork for Elections

Countless individuals have protested and even died to secure the right to vote over the years, but sometimes even a nation's entire population is not enough to preserve that right. Military governments, dictatorships and invading foreign powers often fear democracy and try to snuff it out. In previous centuries, the matter would end in the affected country. But now, thanks to the UN and other regional groups of nations, the world takes on some responsibility in this struggle.

One of the chief roles of the United Nations is to provide peacekeeping forces in troubled parts of the world. Under the leadership of the United Nations, troops from many countries have stepped in to stop fighting and to bring peace to areas of conflict.

But stopping the fighting is often only half the battle. In order to build a lasting peace, UN peacekeeping forces also include police forces, political advisers and experienced observers to guide countries back to a form of representative government. These people often remain in the region long after the fighting has ended. Their successes in places such as Namibia (1989–90), El Salvador (1991–95), and Kosovo (1999–) grab fewer headlines than the frontline fighting, but their work is just as important. International military alliances such as the North Atlantic Treaty Organization (NATO) and regional groups such as the Economic Community of West African States (Ecowas) perform similar roles in bringing stable resolutions to conflicts.

In 1993, the busiest year for UN peacekeepers, the number of peacekeepers deployed – including military and civilian personnel – totalled more than 80,000 people from 77 countries.

Democracy in Haiti

Wealthy countries such as the United States cherish their democratic ideals, but having the right to vote in a poorer country can make the difference between living in poverty and being able to make ends meet. Haiti is a case in point. This Caribbean country is one of the poorest in the world, with land traditionally owned by only a handful of families. The country was formerly ruled by a dictatorship that denied people the right to vote.

In the late 1980s, however, a democracy movement arose in Haiti, forcing the government to call elections. International observers monitored these elections in December 1990, which led to a landslide presidential victory for Jean-Bertrand Aristide, a Roman Catholic priest and an advocate for the poor. The Haitian military then overthrew Aristide and his democratic government. Over the next three years, the UN passed a series of measures calling on member states to use all necessary means, including military force, to restore Haitian democracy. In 1994, the United States sent in 20,000 troops, and the military government stepped down. These US troops were replaced a year later by a UN peacekeeping force, which remained in Haiti for five years until democracy could be restored and maintained.

Unfortunately, Aristide himself was accused of corruption and abuse of power in the next few years, threatening those who opposed him. US troops were once again sent to Haiti in late 2003, and Aristide was forced to leave the country.

Haitian schoolchildren demonstrate in support of Jean-Bertrand Aristide during his first enforced exile in the early 1990s.

9/11 and Democracy

The terrorist attacks in New York and Washington, DC, on September 11, 2001, have been remembered simply as '9/11'. While these numbers reflect the date of the attacks, they also have an additional meaning to Americans, who recognize '911' as the telephone number for emergencies. For many people, the attacks were much more than an unprovoked assault on innocent civilians. They were seen as a blow to the very rights enshrined by political systems that allow debate and protest.

The United States, and the world at large, refrained from taking any sudden retaliation against those people believed to be responsible for the attack. Instead, President George W. Bush examined military information about Al-Qaeda – the terrorist network responsible for the attacks – before declaring a war on terrorism.

A smoky emptiness beyond the Statue of Liberty is all that remained of the Twin Towers of the World Trade Center the day after they were destroyed.

The war had two main purposes. One was to show the pride Americans had in their hard-fought freedoms, especially the right to vote. Many photographs of 9/11 showed the Statue of Liberty in the foreground, with the ruins of the World Trade Center in the distance. This combination of images summed up the determination of the president and the American people to defend democracy against those who they believed would try to destroy it.

The second goal underpinned the American military effort in Afghanistan some months after the attack. It had become apparent that the Taliban, an anti-democratic extremist group ruling Afghanistan, had offered support and military bases to the terrorists. The US military effort in 2002 toppled the Taliban and its supporters, preventing Al-Qaeda from using that country as a haven. Just as importantly, the US military has remained in Afghanistan, to help pave the way for a new, democratically elected government.

A Right or a Duty?

There was concern about the **turnout** in the British general election of 5 May 2005. Many people chose not to vote, some because they had lost trust in Tony Blair's governing Labour party while others disliked the aggressive campaign of the Conservative party. This campaign was masterminded by an Australian political expert, Lynton Crosby, who helped John Howard to victory in Australia in 1998 and 2001.

A few people deciding not to vote can have an enormous effect. The outcome of the 2000 US presidential election was delayed because everything depended on the disputed count in Florida. Only 51 per cent of American voters nationally voted and President George W. Bush's eventual victory depended on just a few hundred votes in a single state.

Throwing Away a Right

Simply throwing away a hard-won right would be a cause for regret. It becomes more serious when we consider how democracies operate. Political leaders will still take office regardless of how many – or few – people actually vote. A candidate could, in theory, persuade a relatively small number of people to vote for him or her. If the candidate did this by stirring up hatred, then the small number of hate-filled voters could become a very powerful force in the country. Some cruel leaders, such as Adolf Hitler in Germany, came to power by taking advantage of such a situation.

Democratic Party National Chairman Terry McAuliffe shares a joke with DJ Biz Markie at a July 2004 party aimed at encouraging youth to vote.

The Youth Vote

People who believe that 'the future of a country is its young people' have begun a number of efforts worldwide to convince

more young people to exercise their democratic right to vote. Supporters of democracy in many countries are concerned that young people feel little attraction for politics and the electoral process. In America, MTV and other youth-orientated media have supported public awareness campaigns such as the Youth Vote Coalition to generate more interest in voting. The future of democracy is indeed in the hands of the new generation of voters. They must, however, realize that they have a duty to exercise their right. If they do, then the long struggle for the right to vote will have succeeded.

Young supporters of the Nazi Party gather in Berlin, Germany, in 1934. Today's young people need to protect their democratic rights by voting if they do not want a return to the horrors of the mid-20th century.

Choosing a winner

A voting system known as 'first past the post' is used in the United Kingdom and in many Commonwealth countries. The British people vote for 646 Members of Parliament (MPs). If 324 or more MPs of a particular party are elected they form an overall majority and that party's leader becomes Prime Minister. But an MP can win election to parliament by just one vote, and a party can gain overall power by winning enough closely-fought contests. A party does not need an overall majority of the votes cast in the country to form a government. In the 2005 election, the Labour party came to power with just over 35 per cent of the national vote.

Likewise, other parties that score well across the country (but not enough to win individual seats) are kept from overall power. Some people want a 'proportional representation' system of voting, which means broadly that each party would have a number of seats in parliament equivalent to the proportion of the votes they obtained. This system would allow smaller parties to gain more MPs, but may prevent one party from taking overall control.

Glossary and Suggested Reading

Amendment   something that is formally added to, or taken away from, an existing document such as the US Constitution

apartheid   a system of laws that separates people according to race

barons   in medieval England, noblemen who held land under a direct grant from the king

bilingual   written in, or understanding, two languages

boycotting   refusing to do business with a person or company as a form of protest

candidate   a person running for elective office

charter   a written document outlining the goals of an organization or country

citizens   natives of a region or country who owe loyalty to it and have specific rights

classes   groups consisting of a number of people who have economic or political characteristics in common

colonies   parts of the world that are governed by a foreign country

communist   a type of government in which the state (government) owns all properties

constitution   a system of principles defining how a country or organization operates

democracy   a form of government in which the people, or their elected representatives, have power

dictatorship   an undemocratic form of government in which a single ruler has virtually total control over a country

estates   the main social divisions of some European countries

executive   the branch of government with supervisory power

fascist   a type of government that calls for national discipline and rule by a powerful dictator

feminists   people who strongly support the rights of women

free press   a system of reporting news events in a country without government interference

General Assembly   the legislature of the United Nations

guillotine   a machine used to execute people by cutting off their heads with a sliding blade

immigration   coming to a new country to settle and live

legislature   the lawmaking branch of government

literacy tests   tests for ability to read or write, often used to deny poorly educated people the chance to vote

Middle Ages   a long period of European history, from the 5th to the 15th centuries

minority   a group that is less than half of a larger group

monarchies   lands ruled by kings or queens

political party   an organized group sharing political goals and offering support to its members when they run for elective office

poll taxes   fees that must be paid in order to qualify to vote

prime minister   the head of government in most countries with parliamentary governments

Puritans   English religious protesters who wanted to purify the Church of England

reason   mental powers used to make judgments or come to conclusions

Reformation   the period beginning in the early 16th century, when some people sought to change (reform) the beliefs and practices of the Catholic Church

republic   a type of government in which representatives are elected to act on behalf of the voters

revolutions   violent overthrows of countries or political systems

Security Council   the division of the United Nations responsible for promoting international peace and consisting of five permanent members (the US , Russia, Britain, France and China) and ten temporary members serving two-year terms

segregation   providing separate facilities and services for members of (usually racially) different groups

suffrage   the right to vote

turnout   the percentage of eligible voters who actually use their vote in an election

treason   betraying one's country, especially by helping that country's enemy

tribunes   officials chosen to defend the rights of the people

tyrants   absolute rulers

unions   groups of people sharing a type of work or employer who band together to press for improved working conditions

Suggested Reading

Adams, Simon. *Winning the Vote.* London and Sydney: Franklin Watts, 2001.

Deary, Terry. *The Knowledge: Party Politics.* London and Sydney: Scholastic, 1996.

Ross, Stewart. *Votes for Women: the Franchise in Britain.* Oxford: Heinemann, 2002.

Saunders, Cheryl. *It's your constitution: governing Australia.* Leichardt, NSW: Federation Press, 1998.

Web Sites

Electoral Commission (UK)
www.electoralcommission.org.uk
Student Virtual Parliament (Australia)
www.studentparliament.net
Young Citizens (UK)
www.youngcitizens.org.uk

Index

Aborigines 27

Afghanistan 43

African-Americans 25, 26, 36, 37

African National Congress (ANC) 35

Alabama 37, 38

Algeria 34

Al-Qaeda 43

American Civil War 25, 26

American Revolution 19

Anthony, Susan B. 29, 31

apartheid 35, 46

Aristide, Jean-Bertrand 42

Australia 22, 27, 31, 39

Britain 4, 12, 14, 15, 16, 17, 18, 22, 24, 28, 30, 31, 34, 39

British Parliament 15, 18, 19, 22, 30

Bush, George W. 43, 44, 45

Canada 22, 27, 31, 39

China 7, 32, 40

colonies 16, 17, 18, 19, 20, 22, 27, 28, 31, 34, 46

communist governments 32–33, 46

Cromwell, Oliver 15
'Declaration of the Rights of Man' 20, 21

democracy 4, 5, 8, 9, 10, 11, 12, 13, 14, 15, 17, 18, 21, 32, 33, 41, 42, 43, 44, 45, 46

dictatorship 9, 33, 41, 42, 46

English Civil War 15, 18

fascist governments 32, 33, 46

feudalism 12

Florida 44, 45

France 8, 12, 16, 18, 20, 21, 22, 29, 34

Freedom Summer 37

French and Indian War 18

French Revolution 20, 21, 29

Gandhi, Mahatma 34

Germany 21, 32, 34, 44

Gouges, Olympe de 29
'The Declaration of the Rights of Women and Citizenesses' 29

grandfather clauses 26

Greece 8, 9, 12, 14

Hitler, Adolf 44

Hussein, Saddam 33

Iceland 13

India 31, 34

Iraq 33

Italy 12, 13, 14, 32

Japan 32, 34

King John I 14, 24

King, Martin Luther, Jr. 38, 39

literacy tests 26, 39, 46

Louis XVI (French king) 20, 21

Magna Carta 14, 24

Malcolm X 38

Mandela, Nelson 34, 35

Massachusetts 17

Mayflower Compact 17, 19

Middle Ages 13, 14, 24, 46

Moses, Bob 37

National Assembly (France) 20, 21

National Union of Woman Suffrage Societies 30

Native Americans 16, 27

Nazi Party 32, 34

New England town meetings 17

New York 31, 37, 43

New Zealand 22, 27, 31

North Atlantic Treaty Organization (NATO) 41

Norway 13, 34

Paine, Thomas 19–20

Pakistan 34

Pankhurst, Emmeline 30

Peterloo Massacre 23

Philippines 31

Pilgrims 17

poll taxes 26, 36, 39, 46

Puritans 17, 47

Reformation 14–15, 47

Reign of Terror 21

Renaissance 14

republic 10, 11, 12–13, 14, 33, 47

Rhode Island 23

Robespierre, Maximilien 21

Rome 9, 10, 11, 12, 14

Russia 25, 26

September 11 attacks 43

serfs 12, 25, 26

slavery 9, 10, 25, 26, 29, 30, 31

South Africa 35

Soviet Union 33

Spain 16, 32

Sparta, Greece 8–9

Stanton, Elizabeth Cady 29

Student Nonviolent Coordinating Committee (SNCC) 37, 38

Taliban 43

Thatcher, Margaret 31

United Nations 40, 41, 42

United States 4, 5, 8, 18, 19, 22, 25, 26, 27, 29, 31, 32, 33, 36, 37, 38, 39, 40, 42, 43, 44, 45

US Congress 4, 27, 39

US Constitution 19, 26, 31, 39
13th Amendment 26
15th Amendment 26
19th Amendment 31
24th Amendment 39
26th Amendment 39

US Declaration of Independence 17, 22, 29

US Supreme Court 38, 45

US Voting Rights Act 37, 39

Vietnam War 39

Virginia 16

Washington, DC 39, 43

Wilson, Woodrow 32

Wollstonecraft, Mary 30
A Vindication of the Rights of Woman 30

woman suffrage 28, 29, 30, 31

Women's Social and Political Union 30

World War I 30, 32

World War II 32, 33, 34, 40

Wyoming 31

Youth Vote Coalition 45

Zimbabwe 33